THE FAVOR OF A WIFE

Healing You to Ignite New Life in Your Marriage

Tabatha Pittman

Copyright © 2021 Tabatha Pittman

All rights reserved. No part of this publication may be reproduced, distributed, or transmitted in any form or by any means, including photocopying, recording, or other electronic or mechanical methods, without the prior written permission of the publisher, except in the case of brief quotations embodied in critical reviews and certain other noncommercial uses permitted by copyright law. For permission requests, write to the publisher, addressed "Attention: Permissions Coordinator," at the email address below.

Email requests to info@TabathaPittman.com.

OrderingInformation:

Quantity sales. Special discounts are available on quantity purchases by corporations, associations, and others. For details, contact the publisher at the email address above.

Published by Tabatha Pittman

Printed in USA

First Printing, 2021

ISBN: 978-1-7356572-2-6

ISBN-13: 978-1-7356572-2-6

DEDICATION

This book is dedicated to You. I exhort you to take deeply to heart what you are about to receive in these chapters. I pray that the gift of wisdom comes in to rest in the midst of your heart, marriage, and home. Lord let your wisdom rest upon the pages of this book and be imparted into every reader who has eyes to see and ears to hear in Jesus name. This book is for every person with a desire for more out of marriage. This book is dedicated to every person who once had a dream of a great marriage but somehow lost that dream because of someone or something. I dedicate this to you because you or someone who loves you invested this book in your life so that you can tap in to The Favor of A Wife!

TABLE OF CONTENT

INTRODUCTION 1
MISCONCEPTION OF MARRIAGE 7
CONFIDENCE, YOUR SILENT WEAPON 15
THE CONFIDENCE PRINCIPLE 20
PRESS PASS THE PAST 25
RESET YOUR MIND 33
WATCH YOUR MOUTH 39
KNOW YOUR WORTH 45
LIST 7 VALUABLE THINGS ABOUT YOURSELF 50

PART TWO

BRING YOUR SEXY BACK 53
BE YOUR OWN COMPETITION 61
CELEBRATE YOUR SCARS 67
LOVE YOURSELF 71

PART THREE

NEVER GIVE IT ONE MORE TRY 77
FREEDOM FROM UNREALISTIC EXPECTATIONS 85
ABOUT THE AUTHOR 92

INTRODUCTION

You may remember how Ne-Yo sang, "Miss Indepent" and talked of how there was just something about her. She had everything and knew how to function without a man. Yes, men desire a woman who is able to be strong and that he can have as his sanctuary. And, I agree that as independent women there are certainly great qualities within. This book is about how the wife, fiancee, can fulfill her marriage by walking in her purpose and focusing on what God says you are: A Wife of Favor.

> *"He who finds a wife finds a good thing, And obtains favor from the Lord."*
>
> Proverbs 18:22

> *A man cannot attain anything better than a good wife. "An excellent wife who can find? She is far more precious than jewels"*
>
> Proverbs 31:10.

TABATHA PITTMAN

You exemplify great competence, noble character and a strong commitment to God and family. You are a priceless gift from God.

You are a favor agent, who unlocks a heightened level of God's grace, mercy, promises and blessings to your spouse. But do you have the keys, the access code to the door?

Early on in my marriage I was overwhelmed by what my family, friends and society deemed correct. I knew what the scripture said but without real life application it was mere memorization. I wanted his love (security) and affection but did not realize he needed me to take action and speak his love language (honor and respect). It took many arguments, counseling appointments, and much prayer to revolutionize my marriage. What did I have to do to break that vicious cycle? The book you have in your hands is The Favor of a Wife about the inner healing I had to undergo to transform my approach to my marriage relationship.

Do you want peace within and at home? Do you want to feel confident and sexy to your spouse? Do you desire to walk in true forgiveness of self and others? Do you want to experience marriage the way God designed it? Then tap into The Favor of a Wife- Healing You to Ignite New Life in Your Marriage!

This book is for anyone: women in marital crisis...wives considering divorce wives in a second marriage wives wanting to stay happily married women trying to heal after divorce engaged women and women desiring marriage coaches and counselors looking for material to help wives save their marriage.

I know that I am promising a lot and I would not share this gudance if I had not fully executed it in my own life. I gained this wisdom by understanding one key scripture that is the foundation of this book.

> *"A wise woman builds her house"*
>
> Proverbs 14:1

Please know that what I am sharing is not a quick fix. Your internal value system was not constructed overnight and thus takes practice to learn and implement new strategies.

The journey to a godly, satisfying marriage is on-going but I have discovered something that can change, strengthen and improve any marriage. I like to call it the vertical and horizontal favor of a wife principle. I see it working in my marriage and I am encountering new blessings as a result. I am therefore charged and have a responsibility to show up as a Naomi to all the Ruth's

TABATHA PITTMAN

who have been found by or are awaiting Boaz. Read on, and I'll show you what I mean.

GOD HAS A PLAN FOR YOU, YOUR MARRIAGE AND YOUR FAMILY.

DO NOT ALLOW ANYONE TO TELL YOU DIFFERENT!

1
MISCONCEPTION OF MARRIAGE

"If you want a pretty dress, and a piece of jewelry call a caterer and have a party but don't get married."

– Juliette Swift

Many times we go through life with an idea of what marriage was supposed to look like from the time we were little girls. We thought we'd grow up have a job, a house, two and half kids, a dog and an awesome marriage to live happily ever after. Maybe your parents had it all together and resembled the Huxtables, the Clevers, the Simpsons or something in between.

Maybe you idealized your parents marriage and wanted to be them, only better. Maybe, you didn't have a marriage mold to follow much less a husband and wife couple to model. Maybe every marriage you saw was a failure and the whole concept was repulsive. Though your thoughts were against marriage, love called and now the altar is summoning your presence. Maybe, like me, you thought you could piece together what you wanted to accomplish in your marriage only to find an element of frustration along the way.

For some reaching these goals is an easy task. For others it is a struggle. Some days are better than others in that we give it the best we have with the tools of fresh vigor each day believing we can conquer the world. Other days we just want to hide out in the bathroom and lock the cares of our heart and head away so we can continue to build a wall between our imaginary marriage and the reality that awaits us. We know what the statistics say about marriage worldwide and the dreadfully alarming statistics of divorce, even in the church. If you are in a place in your marriage life where you feel like gathering bricks or buying bags of cement to seal the deal and run from the true joy of marriage, this book is your manual to stay attentive and awaken the passion within you so that you can enjoy the fruit of your labor and the joy of building a beautiful life with your spouse all over again from the inside out.

No more hoping and wishing, and looking for the spark in your marriage to magically reappear. No more wishing for the man you fell in love with, long before his every move annoyed you to your wits end. No more kicking yourself thinking you married the wrong person and the grass must be greener on the other side, when its actually astroturf. No more dreaming of a better marriage to someone else! No more believing the lies or fairytales. This is not Cinderella and there is no Prince Charming. This is life and it is meant to be lived with zeal, hope, and purpose. Your marriage has purpose and giving up is not the answer. No more sleeping on true happiness that is designed for your marriage! No more sleeping on the motivation, ambition, and vision required for you to have a successful marriage! It's time for the vital knowledge for your marriage to collide with God's desire and it's time for you to WAKE UP

THE FAVOR OF A WIFE WITHIN YOU!

My good friend Linda, who's parents were married 45 years, told me the story of how her father, Mr. Swift would say, "There are three things you have got to know you cannot half do: God, Marriage, and raising kids." Mr. Swift was in effect saying that you have got to give it your all. Marriage is not a 50/50 situation, equation or chance. Marriage requires that two whole people show up 100:100. You have to be Committed. I have heard it said that, "A great marriage does not happen because of the love you had in the beginning but how well you continue building love until the end."

The following are a set of declarations I created to accompany and affirm you along your journey. One of the easiest and most fruitful ways to become a wife of noble character is to repeatedly speak it over yourself, preferably out loud.

A WIFE'S DECLARATION

I AM A WOMAN WHO IS ENJOYED

I AM A WOMAN WHO IS GRACIOUS

I AM A WOMAN WHO BRINGS HAPPINESS

I AM SUCCESSFUL BEYOND MEASURE!

I AM A PLEASANT WOMAN

I AM A BEAUTIFUL AND RARE JEWEL

I AM WHAT IS GOOD TO MY HUSBAND (FUTURE HUSBAND) AND CHILDREN (FUTURE CHILDREN).

I SEEK THE TRUTH, WAY AND LIGHT.

I WALK IN THE TRUTH FOR MY HOUSEHOLD AND MARRIAGE

I CREATE A LOVING ENVIRONMENT IN MY MARRIAGE, FAMILY AND HOME

I CREATE AN AUTHENTIC AND INTIMATE RELATIONSHIP WITH JESUS

TABATHA PITTMAN

I AM A WIFE WHO SPEAKS WITH WISDOM AND ALWAYS UPLIFTS MY HUSBAND

I AM A GOD FEARING WOMAN WHO LIVES WITH A POSITIVE AND LOVING ATTITUDE I AM THE BEST WIFE MY HUSBAND COULD EVER DREAM OF

I AM A WOMAN WHO IS TRANSFORMED DAILY BY THE RENEWING OF MY THOUGHTS

I SPEAK SUCCESSFUL LIFE GIVING WORDS AND I MAKE SUCCESSFUL DECISIONS

I CONNECT WITH OTHER LOVING AND GOD FEARING WOMEN

I AM BEAUTIFUL

I AM CLASSY

I AM ELEGANT

I REPEL AVERAGE BECAUSE I WAS CREATED TO BE EXCELLENT.

THE FAVOR OF A WIFE

I AM THE GREATEST PRAYER WARRIOR AND I GO TO BATTLE BOLDY AND DAILY ON BEHALF OF MYSELF, MY HUSBAND AND MY CHILDREN.

I ATTRACT FAVOR

SPIRITUALLY, MENTALLY, PHYSICALLY AND FINANCIALLY.

I SPEAK TO THE CORE OF WHO I AM AND I SAY TO MYSELF AND THOSE WHO ARE AROUND ME....
I AM A WIFE OF FAVOR!

2
CONFIDENCE, YOUR SILENT WEAPON

"Confidence is that feeling by which the mind embarks in great and honorable courses with a sure hope and trust in itself."

– Cicero

Hopes, ambitions, having a successful marriage, fulfilling purpose becomes bedridden from the start when you possess no confidence to embark on the journey. It is good to be filled with hopes and aspirations, but when you start the journey without confidence, your hopes become paralyzed, and your aspirations do not lead your mind to become a reality.

Being a reflective person, you might have taken the pain to sit and reflect on how far you have come in life, what you are lacking, what led to where you are, and many other questions that storm your mind. A point that might entirely slip your mind is the condition of your confidence.

TABATHA PITTMAN

Some situations occur in life that drains you of energy, vibe, and strength to forge ahead. Amidst all these is your confidence, waning. When life happens, if there is anything you need to revive, it is your confidence. Life might not have smiled on you so far; in fact, you might not have enjoyed or experienced sweetness in your journey on planet earth, but a sure thing you can do, is never to drown your confidence.

Your confidence is your silent weapon. It is a silent weapon to you, but it is on the loudest volume to people around you when you wear it. Your confidence is your strength and power of influence. It can buy you anything, and you can sell anything with it. If you don't possess anything, your confidence can buy you everything. You cannot undermine or underestimate the power of confidence, and that is why it must not be drowned. Find your healing by starting to give expression to your confidence.

When life's struggles begin to wear you down, your dreams seem out of reach, hopes away from you, your start-up energy to regain all you've lost is your confidence. You might not have everything, but when your confidence is revived, it is an inexcusable glow that drips of positivity and possibility.

It is easier to achieve in life when you wear your confidence. It proclaims you to the world. It tells everyone you meet that you are different! You are extraordinary, regardless of your background or experience in life.

> "but those who hope in the Lord will renew their strength. They will soar on wings like eagles; they will run and not grow weary, they will walk and not be faint."
>
> Isaiah 40:31

As a Christian, there is a type of confidence that springs from trusting the Lord and His word; it is different from self-confidence. It is a confidence that comes when you have an unfailing supernatural power that you rely on. This kind of confidence is not bought. It comes by trusting God.

On the one hand, the above scriptures tell you what should happen. In reality, your strength can waiver. When the cares of life, no matter your status, has had you running you are bound to grow weary. If you walk long enough in your strength, you will become faint. The same concept is also applicable to our lives. There are situations in life that require us to walk, and when we walk for long with a matter on our heart, we become faint. Our hope becomes slim and the spark to go on begins to dwindle.

TABATHA PITTMAN

At a stage in our lives, we begin to run, run to get riches, have properties, excel in a career, and have a good marriage. When we run after these things, and it doesn't seem to be working the way we planned or envisioned it, we become weary—no strength left to carry on.

But this is the word of God, it says those who hope in the Lord, whose trust is forever in Him, their strength will be renewed! The reality of fainting and being wearied, which is natural human frailty, would no more be present in their lives. Instead of walking and running, they soar like eagles. This sort of strength can only be from God.

If God says you will soar above your disappointment, failings, fears, weakness, losses, then believe Him for His word! You cannot wear better confidence than that which the Lord says to you! Get God's word into your system and wear it everywhere you go! Be known for what the Lord says, not what your circumstance says.

> *"For you created my inmost being; you knit me together in my mother's womb. I praise you because I am fearfully and wonderfully made; your works are wonderful, I know that full well."*

THE FAVOR OF A WIFE

Psalm 139:13–14

There are times that we spend our all on a course because we want to see it being fruitful. Commit to it. We commit to our marriage, give our all to make it work, work on ourselves, and work on our partners, but it seems things are not just in shape yet. Sometimes, it's even worse. We become emotionally, psychologically, financially, and spiritually drained.

The one and the only hope is God, and it is more to our advantage if we put our total trust in Him. How wonderful it is to be fully assured in God's word! It is priceless. It is far beyond self-confidence or assurance. Meditate on God's word to bring out your confidence and exhibit this confidence wherever you find yourself. It is your silent weapon.

> **IF YOU GOT MARRIED TO GET YOUR NEEDS MET, YOU ARE GOING TO GET DIVORCED. MARRIAGE IS TO MEET THE NEEDS OF YOUR SPOUSE**

THE CONFIDENCE PRINCIPLE

Being a Wife of Favor is about learning to live intentionally by learning to love purposefully. This all begins with **THE CONFIDENCE PRINCIPLE**. It will help you reclaim focus on the person that matters most during the process of healing you and walking in the Favor of a Wife, and that person is YOU! When your relationship with YOU is not in the right position, it opens the door for an unfit balance in your connection with others and especially your spouse.

The focus of this principle is to assist you with learning the importance of loving yourself again. This is about seeing you the way God sees you. Ask God to show you the _____ (insert your name here) that He sees. You are unique and there is no other human being on this planet designed and created to be like you. When you spend time loving who you are, you won't have time hating on or comparing yourself to any others in your peripheral view.

3 Ways to Have Confidence in God:

Confidence in the spirit. It's a daily battle to surrender the flesh and to walk in the Spirit, but doing so, will build your confidence away from the flesh and into the spirit.

> *"For the flesh desires what is contrary to the Spirit and the Spirit what is contrary to the flesh. They are in conflict with each other, so that you are not to do whatever you want."*
>
> —Galatians 5:17

Confidence in who You are. Find confidence through resting in Him. By having total faith and confidence in God, we can trust He knew what He was doing when he made us. And we can have confidence in the beauty of His creation.

> *"But blessed is the one who trusts in the Lord, whose confidence is in him"*
>
> Jeremiah 17:7

Confidence in our Heavenly Father and Jesus. I pray you realize how your confidence has built over time by simply

TABATHA PITTMAN

surrendering to the Lord, rejoicing in what the day will bring, and delighting in being the salt of the earth, and light of the world.

> *"Let us then approach God's throne of grace with confidence, so that we may receive mercy and find grace to help us in our time of need."*
>
> —Hebrews 4:16

God writes clearly that confidence is secured in Christ, and that we can have it to the fullest. "The fruit of that righteousness will be peace; its effect will be quietness and confidence forever."

Isaiah 32:17

"Confidence is Your Portion"

~

Tabatha Pittman

3
PRESS PASS THE PAST

"The past can't hurt you anymore, not unless you let it."

— Alan Moore

Of a truth, the past may hurt, but it can only hurt when you allow it. Every decision and action has its own consequences. Now, no matter the consequence that might have hit you and caused pain in your life, you can allow it to continue if you let it permeate into your present. Meaning you have a choice in the matter. You can choose to waddle in the consequence or dust yourself off and try again.

Mistakes are lessons, and so are the circumstance that you found yourself in the past. The woman you once were weeks, months, and years ago cannot define your present. Your past doesn't control or determine your present unless you allow it.

A gift you can adorably give yourself is the gift of letting go. In many cases of letting go of the past, you might need to forgive yourself for the mistakes or forgive others who have hurt you. There is no grievance that cannot be forgiven. If the good Lord could give himself, carry the punishment of the world's sin and remit it with His own blood, He can give you the grace to forgive all the hurt people have caused you.

Forgiveness is a choice and a process. We must engage in this exercise, consciously and daily. If there is an ex-boyfriend, or ex-husband, or even a family member, forgive them so you can flourish. Let go of the pain, and the memories that tend to hold you hostage with lock and key in your mind. Forgiveness is an act of faith. It is not a feeling, and if our forgiveness is contingent on a feeling you may never feel like forgiving them. Deal with your feelings later, but forgive them now so that you can move on from that situation.**Remember forgiveness is for you.**

Forgive. It is a decision you must make to live in true freedom. Freedom to love yourself and others requires forgiveness. This is part of the healing process so that you can be the favor agent God has called you to be as a wife.

In essence, the pressure of the past is not needed in the vision you've created in your mind for your purpose, home, ministry, career, business, finance, and every other aspect of your life. You can still be the woman God wants you to be.

THE FAVOR OF A WIFE

Regardless of your past, position, status, family, or race. God is interested in every bit of you, and you can start getting your healing by pressing pass the past.

Getting entangled with the past is a self-destructive mechanism. No one moves forward nor gains momentum while holding on to the past. The hurts might come calling, a new wave of pain and distress, surges of anxiety and uncertainty, but this is all the past will ever bring. It doesn't bring progress, success, achievement, and peace, a blissful home, a fulfilling career, or ministry.

> *"When we think we have been hurt by someone in the past, we build up defenses to protect ourselves from being hurt in the future. So the fearful past causes a fearful future, and the past and future become one. We cannot love when we feel fear.... When we release the fearful past and forgive everyone, we will experience total love and oneness with all."*
>
> — Gerald G. Jampolsky

Simply put, nothing good comes from regurgitating the past. The past should be put in the past, and left behind you. My grandmother would say it this way, "let dead dogs lie." Do not allow anyone to drag your past into your present. Remember satan comes to steal, kill, and destroy (John 10:10) and he always deals in your past. You are in the best place to control what comes and stays on your mind. Be conscious of your thought life, and don't allow it to dwell on the past. Choose to press forward and move on.

> *"Forget the former things; do not dwell on the past. See, I am doing a new thing! Now it springs up; do you not perceive it? I am making a way in the wilderness and streams in the wasteland."*
>
> —Isaiah 43:18-19

It is more refreshing to release yourself to God for complete healing. He knows you, even before you were conceived, He thought of you and had you in mind. He is aware of your past and current struggles. None of what has happened to you is hidden from Him. He is a father who knows the exact care His child needs.

You need to release your heart to God for healing. He will help you to forgive easily. He will caress your heart and heal you of every pain. Satan will deter you, try to stop you by reminding you how much pain you were caused and how you can't forgive. Know that it is utterly a lie. Don't give in to your past. The Lord is making a way in the wilderness and water in the desert. He is making the impossible possible.

The above verses say you should forget the former things. Don't dwell on it because God is springing up a big surprise for you! A new thing is coming your way! That is God's word for you! Let your heart be ready to receive all that the Lord has in store for you, and God shall transform your life.

THE TRANSFORMATION PRINCIPLE

The Transformation Principle is a Christ-centered, Bible based approach to changing your thought life. God's word can can break self-destructive thought patterns that rob you of living a joyful, healthy and whole life. When we meditate on the Word of God day and night and write it on the tablets of our heart it takes root in our heart and soul. I say to you where light is darkness cannot coexist.

> *"And be not conformed to this world: but be ye transformed by the renewing of your mind, that ye may prove what is that good, and acceptable, and perfect, will of God."*
>
> Roman 12:2

TABATHA PITTMAN

Though I have read that scripture seemingly a thousand times, it holds new revelation for me each and every time and stage of my life. It reminds me of the metamorphosis that a butterfly goes through. It starts as a caterpillar, on its belly slivering and eating off of the foliage. A small known fact is that in this stage it only consumes and cannot produce. At this stage it also has to watch for predators who prey on it's lowly state. This phase may last up to a year. Perhaps your year has been stretched out or condensed but know it is all part of the process. Maybe that's where you are in the state of your mind toward trying to solve problems within or inside your marriage.

Then it goes through the cocoon phase, which is a lot less glamorous. During this stage the casing develops and envelopes a cycle of darkness that is necessary to mature, change and prepare. Prepare for the greater. The Bible is filled with stories of men and women who had to go through cocoons of some sort, one way or the other. Beyond a shadow of a doubt the message is the same, your transformation will take time. I have had to transform my thought life from unworthy thoughts, self sabotage, comparing, and insecurity. I can testify that it did not happen over night. However, when I surrendered my thoughts to Christ I was able to stand boldy and confidently and allow His strength to be made perfect in my weakness. The cocoon stage is cultivating and making you. Let me be the first to witness that the prep time was well worth knowing that I do not have to rely on worldy wisdom or be the self-reliant independent woman that is touted as a she-ro in modern day society. I quickly learned the independent woman must give way to submit and yield to my husband in order to soar in my marriage.

The emergence of the butterfly breaking through the hard shell of the cocoon is the true story of Jesus being the author and finisher of your faith. He knows your beginning from the end. When you invite him in to live and nurture a relationship it is true discovery of your souls purpose. There is purpose for your life as a wife, mother, in your education and career. Take heart that you are covered because you surrendered the past to embrace the purpose. The purpose God has for your life to give you hope and a future. The purpose of seeing you flourish and spread your wings as a woman of excellence and noble character. Arise as a spiritually healthy overcoming woman united for your purpose (S.H.O.W.U.P.), and fully operating in the gifts handcrafted for your life.

"We do not heal the past
by dwelling there;
We heal the past
by living fully in the present."

Marianne Williamson

4
RESET YOUR MIND

"Once your mindset changes, everything on the outside will change along with it."

~Steve Maraboli

The state of your mind matters and determines who you become. The produce of your mind, which are your thoughts, play a huge part in determining what you receive out of life. It's like a seed; when sown, it produces fruit. The fruits are what you make out of life. You will know the root by the fruit.

A mind is a place of decision making. The activities that take place in your mind affect what you get in reality. You might not necessarily have a faulted or negative mind. However, if your mind is unproductive then the source of your ideas and strategic planning is unproductive, it will definitely affect your reality.

There is a need to set your mind in the right shape and good balance as a woman. Ask yourself; what do I feed my mind? Is my mind always appreciative or condemning? Am I positive in my perspective towards life and people or negative? What reaction do I give off? These questions aid you to know the state of your mind and the kind of person you are.

Your reaction to the situation going on around you, your marriage, in the lives of your children, your workplace, your ministry, your extended family depends on your perspective and mindset about them.

As a woman who wants to maximize our strength and see every endeavor working out, our mindset is the preliminary stage where everything must be right. If you don't have the right perspective, you won't be happy with the result you get. The saying perception is everything, rings true.

Take a corrective measure and start to assess your life in a new light. Reject degrading thoughts and consciously stay on positive ones. Your thoughts shouldn't cast you down. If you experience a bad situation, but your mind is positive, the effect of the situation won't weigh you down from forging ahead.

> *"I destroy every claim and every reason that keeps people from knowing God. I keep every thought under control in order to make it obey Christ."*
>
> 2 Corinthians 10:5

THE FAVOR OF A WIFE

The Bible tells us to take every thought captive. That means that I have a chance to do something about all thoughts that are not well-pleasing to God, before they enter my heart and become a part of me!

> *"As a man thinks, so is he."*
>
> Proverbs 23:7

What we think about is crucial to who we are. The minds of some people do not perceive anything good. They are mostly filled with complaint and grudges. This does not bring progress to one's life or family. Things work together by starting with the right mindset. Take your mind away from hurts or things of the past. Be resilient in making your life better.

> *"Do not conform to the pattern of this world, but be transformed by the renewing of your mind. Then you will be able to test and approve what God's will is—his good, pleasing and perfect will ."*
>
> Romans 12:2

TABATHA PITTMAN

The Bible says our minds need renewal. We are in the world but not of the world. Our minds should not be patterned according to the events going on in this world. You can only become transformed in mind and reality when you renew your mind. Change your perspective. Being able to discern the good, pleasing, and perfect will of God for your life is especially important.

Without knowing and approving God's perfect will for your life, it is like walking on earth without a compass. Without a purpose. Realize the importance of your mind in your life and home. Know that without resetting your mind to align with God's purpose for your life and marriage, you won't be able to get the best out of life. Be transformed into the woman God has purposed you to be by daily renewing your mind and aligning to God's will for you.

As women who are ready, willing, able and committed to healing from the inside out and tapping into The Favor Of A Wife, resetting your mindset for the level of greatness you are about to enter is important. Once your mindset changes, everything on the outside will change along with it. Trying to enter a new arena of your life with an old mindset will lead you right back into the problems you are presently facing, a rut. So a change has to occur. Realize that the enemy does not like marriage, and does not want you to walk in your purpose as a woman and wife. But the devil is a LIAR. Your mind is renewed daily. The battle is for your mind and You Win!

> Reset your mindset and realize that you don't have problems, you have opportunities to grow together in your marriage.

"Nothing Increases Your Progress Like A Positive Mindset."

~

Tabatha Pittman

5
WATCH YOUR MOUTH

> "Respect is the language a man understands."
>
> ~ Dr. Emmerson Eggerichs

Confession is said to be possession. The mouth is an important vessel in the life of a man because whatever you say is what you will eventually become. Your mind first conceives the idea of what you want; the confession of it shapes your reality. If you conceive in your mind that you want to be successful, you begin to work towards it and say it; by so doing, you are aligning your thought with the words of your mouth. Said differently, whatever you describe you prescribe. Meaning, your words have power and the ability to tell your subsconscious mind to create, for better or worse.

An African adage says, 'the voice is an egg; when it falls, it can't form into an egg anymore." This is to say that immediately upon speaking a word, the impact is forever, and it can't be retrieved or retracted. If it is positive, the effect is good; if it is negative, the damage is done. That is why some relationships become shipwrecked when the individuals piloting them aren't careful with the words of their mouth. I remember doing an exercise with a women's Bible study group. In groups of two or three we were given a bowl and a tube of toothpaste. Each lady was alotted a couple minutes to speak. As she spoke the others squeezed the toothpaste into the bowl. The instructor then said now try to put the toothpaste back in the tube. It was impossible. Likewise, our words have lasting effects that cannot be undone.

> *"For, "Whoever would love life and see good days must keep their tongue from evil and their lips from deceitful speech."*
>
> 1Peter 3:10

The Bible emphasizes the effect of the words that come out of our mouths and how it can cost a lifetime change. It is advised in the above verse that whoever wants to see good days on this earth should keep their tongue from evil. Sometimes when you're tired of the situation, you begins to think of a negative outcome. One might even wish that evil should happen to one, but this should not be the case. Don't speak evil to yourself; don't speak evil concerning others. Your words have power.

THE FAVOR OF A WIFE

A deceitful woman is not a virtuous woman. When you begin to tell lies and deceive yourself, thinking you are deceiving others, your days won't be pleasant because when the truth comes out, you will keep reaping what you have sown. As a matter of fact, there is nothing you will gain by deceiving people. You only put pressure on yourself to impress others; how comfortable is that? It is like trying to put on a dress that's too small for you; or walking around in shoes that don't fit because you want to win and impress people.

> *Be comfortable in your own skin; no one can make you be what you don't want to be. Be loyal to your spouse and the people around you. It is a sense of accountability.*
>
> Proverbs 10:19

"Too much talk leads to sin, be sensible and keep your mouth shut."

Some women have been labeled talkative. Some won't even know that all the details of their lives have been spilled out to strangers. A woman should know what details of her life and family she wants others to know about. When you talk too much, you will unknowingly add subtle lies to it, and it becomes sin. Be watchful; it is not necessary for the whole world to know everything about you, nor every thought that comes to your mind. Don't tell the details of your home life to the enemy because of your talkativeness. Mind what you say and watch your mouth, because the enemy is listening. I liken this to those who "overshare" on social media. All of your business is in a post, everytime there is good or bad going on in your relationship. Be mindful of putting all your business out there verbally or socially.

> *"Let your conversation be always full of grace, seasoned with salt, so that you may know how to answer everyone."*
>
> Colossians 4:6

The above verse is a secret that has kept several marriages. As an individual, if you are mindful of what you say, it will be easy for you to clarify yourself and know the right answer to give when you are being quoted. Let the words of your mouth be edifying to lives around you. It is by the words of your mouth that you will be known. I'm not saying you have to be a mute, but in the words of Kenny Rogers, "You got to know when to hold 'em, know when to fold 'em." Talk when you are supposed to and when you need to stand up for right. Talk and let it be seasoned with salt so that your words hold weight and aren't empty dialogue.

THE FAVOR OF A WIFE

"Do not let any unwholesome talk come out of your mouths, but only what is helpful for building others up according to their needs, that it may benefit those who listen."

Ephesians 4:29

Keep your mouth intact. The world shouldn't influence your attitude, you should influence the world with your right attitude.

"If we understood the power of our thoughts, we would guard them more closely. If we understood the awesome power of our words, we would prefer silence to almost anything negative. In our thoughts and words, we create our own weaknesses and our own strengths. Our limitations and joys begin in our hearts. We can always replace negative with positive."

Betty Eadie

"Death and life are in the power of the tongue: and they that love it shall eat the fruit thereof."

Proverbs 18:21

6
KNOW YOUR WORTH

"What lies behind us and what lies before us are tiny matters compared to what lies within us."

Ralph Waldo Emerson

As women who have made contributions in societies since the beginning of time, we begin to add value to ourselves as we grow into adulthood. Either by what we do, a skill we acquire, connections we have, impacts we make, and several other things that boost our self-esteem.

We carry our value into the friendships and relationships that we make, and one way or the other, it influences our decisions. Our self-worth matters to us because it's a direct interpretation of our essence. It tells people how significant you are and how much you appreciate yourself. Your self worth allows you to stand up and teach people how to treat you. Your self worth also establishes boundaries as you confidently convey your principles to others.

TABATHA PITTMAN

It is beautiful when you see yourself adding value. You are an asset that appreciate more; you become indispensable in whatever sphere you find yourself. As important as it is to have self-worth, some circumstances and relationships can drain your self-worth. In the case of emotionally invested relationships that turn abusive, its first effect on the individual being abused is to drown his/her self-worth.

You might have invested your all in your past relationships and have gotten nothing out of it other than ridicule and abuse. There is much more you can do in this process of healing. God can pick up your broken pieces and make a masterpiece out of them. He can turn nothing into something. Turn your bad breaks into a breakthrough.

That is more reason that your past should be left in the past. It shouldn't speak or influence your future. The Bible says a person in Christ is a new creature; old things are passed away; behold, all things are new. Let your brand new self emerge. The old things have been done away with.

You are the sole determinant of what you get out of life. If your past still dictates your present or future, it is totally wrong. Be determined to grow above low self-esteem and don't allow what people say to affect you. Do not give people power they

THE FAVOR OF A WIFE

have neither earned nor deserve; and stop letting people who do not matter to much, matter too much.

Surround yourself with people who are positively and purposely driven. Stay away from those who are filled with negativity. All they do is act and say negative things. They see nothing good in any situation. We must protect our ear gates, because we know faith comes by hearing.

> *For the Spirit God gave us does not make us timid, but gives us power, love and self-discipline.*
>
> 2 Timothy 1:7

Most importantly, let the word of God mold you. Let it build you. Let it be your confidence. Feed and meditate on God's word; it is the greatest energy and morale booster you can ever have.

Don't let anyone put or pull you down. Don't let anyone injure you with the words of their mouth. Be diligent to know what people say in your life and be responsible for the relationships you keep.

TABATHA PITTMAN

I encourage you to build a Careforce. Your Careforce should be people you trust and allow to hold you up with encouragement and build you up with accountability to be your best self. This team is designated to intercede, sow, minister and/or mentor you in good and bad times so you can grow and go higher in your calling as a woman and a wife. They are here to remind you of the value you bring when your motivation slacks.

Nothing is more important than knowing your value because everything comes into clear view when you do.

> *But we have this treasure in earthen vessels, that the Excellency of the power may be of God, and not of us.*
>
> 2 Corinthians 4:7

You are valuable, a treasure, and priceless in God's sight. It does not matter how great your outfit is, the price of your red bottom shoes, or how flawless your makeup and hair; if you do not value what, who, and whose you are on the inside. Making yourself beautiful on the outside is not a substitute for knowing the content on the inside. It's like a pretty box that is empty. As a wife of favor, you cannot afford to be walking around seemingly having it all together but devoid of presence and worth. Empty people aren't content because they have no content. Choose today to start valuing yourself.

KNOW YOURSELF

You must define and value yourself. Once you do that everything else will fall into its rightful place. You are very important and the best part is that your value increases each day you embrace that realization. Realize that everything about you matters. You are not what people try to label you as when they do not know the value of what is inside of you. They do not know your backstory or what you had to go through to get here. This is why declarations were created so you can speak life into your life. So you can do as God told Job and command your morning. I want to assist you in the development of knowing who you are. You are royalty, you are beautiful and you are excellence embodied. Be happy and comfortable with who you are and refuse to compare or compete with anyone else.

Aspire to higher things and respect yourself enough to walk away from anything or anyone that devalues you or makes you lose your happiness. Daily make a conscience efforts to value yourself and not rely on others to determine your worth. How you value yourself shows up in every area of your life be it positive or negative.

LIST 7 VALUABLE THINGS ABOUT YOURSELF

1. _____

2. _____

3. _____

4. _____

5. _____

6. _____

7. _____

"When you force yourself to try to be like anyone other than your unique self, you will not operate in your true identity."

~

Tabatha Pittman

PART TWO

The Outer Woman

7

BRING YOUR SEXY BACK

> *"Sexiness is a state of mind - a comfortable state of being. It's about loving yourself in your most unlovable moments."*
>
> -Halle Berry

In the world where we are, there are different definitions that portray the act of being sexy. Many ladies wear what they wear because they want to be tagged sexy. Naturally, the feminine power is embedded so that a woman can effortlessly attract the opposite sex. It is not the low cut blouse baring cleavage, or the skin tight dress that should define being sexy.

Taking care of your appearance and dressing appropriately is the ultimate sexy, no matter what the number is on the tag or the scale. As women we are naturally alluring. God divinenly embedded the power in a woman to cause and hold attraction. It is an aura, a demeanor that is written all over you.

TABATHA PITTMAN

Wearing your sexiness includes bringing on your confidence, self-worth, being hardworking, disciplined, and courageous. It is you being comfortable in your own skin. It is you being you no matter the circumstance you find yourself in. It is you being modest and alluring at the same time. It is you showing courtesy and respect. It is you respecting other people's views and not compelling them to your own conviction.

It is you dressing gorgeously and honorably. It is you being at the reins of your affairs. It is you projecting your womanhood in all its positivity. It is you exhibiting godly virtues. It is you knowing what to say and when to say it, as well as how to say it. You can see that there is a lot to you being sexy. It is you being a pretty and prudent woman.

You can't possess this sexiness without being alluring to the men. You become irresistible to your spouse. It is important that you take good care of your appearance. And not only your appearance, add value to yourself. Be of inestimable value! That is sexier!

> *"The girl had a beautiful figure and was lovely to look at."*
>
> Esther 2:7

THE FAVOR OF A WIFE

This is Esther; her shape was well noticed that it was included in her description. In the present world, it would have been described as being 'curvy.' Esther was a brick house. Her figure was beautiful to behold, and to add to it; she is lovely to look at. This simply means you might be tempted at her appearance because she was such a beauty to behold. If Esther, during her time, could be described like this, how much more should you?

> *"Before a young woman's turn came to go in to King Xerxes, she had to complete twelve months of beauty treatments prescribed for the women, six months with oil of myrrh and six with perfumes and cosmetics."*
>
> Esther 2:12

Can you see how painstakingly the women were treated just to appear before the King? If you have the resources, you can regularly give yourself a spa treatment. Look good, always. Smell nice; it is not a sin. Wear a nice perfume that does not enter before you do but leaves a sweet fragrance wafting in the air. I believe every woman should have a signature fragrance, your go to scent. Take care of your body. Exercise. Your health is your wealth. You do not have to have a membership to the gym to workout. You can do walking videos from the internet. This is all about being intentional to take care of your body, you only get one. Eat mindfully so that you feel good about you inside and out. I have often shared with women that your lifestyle (not diet) is 80% what you eat and 20% of what you do. That being said eat in a way that yields energy and not sluggishness. (There is grace for the holiday feast) Lastly, spend time with yourself. Get to know YOU better. This includes making quiet time to prioritize YOU. I like to fill my time with prayer, meditation and soaking in the presence of the Lord. When I emerge I am rejuvenated, and ready to run the course as a wife, mother, and entrepreneur.

> *"The woman was very beautiful, a virgin; no man had ever slept with her."*
>
> Genesis 24:16

This is not an outdated sexiness. Chastity is sexy. As an unmarried lady, nothing is sexier than keeping your body just as God's word instructed. The Bible says the marriage bed should be undefiled, both before and after marriage. No shade to those who have had premarital sex. But I want to encourage you that your body is a temple keep it clean by abstaining.

THE FAVOR OF A WIFE

The Songs of Solomon chapter 4 extravagantly describe the sexiness of King Solomon's bride given by King Solomon himself.

> "Your lips are like a scarlet thread, and your mouth is lovely. Your cheeks are like halves of a pomegranate behind your veil. Your hair is like a flock of goat leaping down the slopes of Gilead."
>
> Song of Solomon 4: 3

> "Your lips drip nectar, my bride; honey and milk are under your tongue; the fragrance of your garments is like the fragrance of Lebanon."
>
> Song of Solomon 4:11

This shows that men appreciate their women dripping hot. You look irresistible to them. Look neat. Let your environment speak neatness. Awaken your sexuality. If you are married, spice up your romance. Let your spouse know you are as hot as when he met you, and you are going to hold his attraction and attention forever.

While on this topic, allow me to introduce another aspect of the Favor of a Wife, being sensual: Sexual Intelligence. Much like emotional intelligence that women often want men to exercise, is the sexual intelligence quotient. Marty Klein, Ph.D, renowned sex therapist said, "sexual intelligence is expressed in the ability to create and maintain desire in a situation that's less than perfect or comfortable; the capacity to adapt to your changing body; curiosity and open-mindedness about the meaning of pleasure, closeness, and satisfaction; and the ability to adjust when things don't go as expected." Stated another way sexual intelligence is knowing your body, understanding your desires, being safe and relaxed to explore sexual experiences. In my opinion, wives are to value and prioritize the physical desires of their husband. Here are a few actions/attitudes a wife can take toward her husbands sexuality:

1. Do not shame your husband for sexuality, it is a gift from God. (treat it accordingly)

2. Dress in a way your husband finds sexy and extenuates the body God gave you. (Men are visual)

3. Recognize that there will be times your feelings match your sexual actions and sometimes they will not. Aka when you don't feel like it. However, breaking out of the sexual comfort zone may ignite a more passionate marriage.

THE FAVOR OF A WIFE

Remember this is about you bringing your sexy back. Internally igniting confidence and feeling good about yourself. Be bold and brave in and out of the bedroom. Sex is much more than just a physical act it is a release, a connection, a way to express desire, a form of worship, and a culmination of love.

"Sexual Intelligence requires that a wife takes action and a right attitude toward her husband's sexuality."

~

Tabatha Pittman

8

BE YOUR OWN COMPETITION

"The toughest competition is competing with yourself – to try to be better than what you have performed or achieved."

Dr T.P.Chia

Right from birth we experience different cases of competition. That girl in the neighborhood, the one at school, college, at the workplace, she gave you reasons to compete. Sometimes they even throw the signs of inviting you into competition with them.

In life, we all tread different paths. Events that will occur to Ms. A are different from Ms. B. There might be similar experiences, but they can never occur the same way. We are unique in our different ways. That is why our lives cannot be lived the same way. We are different people with different interests.

There are observed cases of competition between businesses, ministries, and families, to say the least. There are unhealthy rivalries that basically don't bring progress. It impedes the other individual. This is not the kind of competition being discussed here.

Being in competition with yourself removes the chance of having a rival. You become your own rival because you want to see a better you. When you compete with yourself, it means you have seen the need for improvement. In your marriage, finance, career, business, ministry, you become a better you everyday.

Seeing the need to rise to the challenge of improving each day as a well-rounded woman, you do not rest in complacency. You understand that complacency is the enemy of progress. You begin to work your way to improvement. How do you start the race to be in competition with yourself?

First, you must be focused on improving yourself. Know that no one is in competition with you other than yourself. This is your self-improvement stage. You may have a model, but they aren't your definite end. You can be better than them. It depends on how much hard work and learned experiences you go through. That is to say how many lessons you actually take into account to grow and learn. How many obstacles have now become stepping stones to your future. Better still, how many

THE FAVOR OF A WIFE

opportunities has life provided you to show resiliency and overcome.

Let your goals be your watchword. At this junction, you need to envision what you want to achieve with your life and plan it out. Write it out. Work on it. Work with it. Having dreams and aspirations are not enough to fulfill them. You may have great plans and ideas, don't let it stop at conception. It can become a reality if you write it down and work towards achieving it.

> "Then the LORD replied: "Write down the revelation and make it plain on tablets so that a herald may run with it."
>
> Habakkuk 2:2-3

This will always be in light of what interests you, what you can do over and over without being tired of it. Even when you are tired phsyically, you will still find the strength to accomplish these goals. What are your goals for your marriage, finance, children, career, business, and all other aspects of your life? What commitments have you made towards making your home a sanctuary of peace?

Write your concerns and how you plan to work them out. Immediately you start out on improving, occasionally track your success and always give thanks. Celebrate your accomplishments, big and small, in a way that allows you to elevate and motivates you to the next goal. Appreciate or commend yourself when needed and note other things that still need progress.

At this point, know that not all opinions count. Don't hold tight to people's opinions, especially if they are negative. Believe in yourself and in what you are capable of doing. Don't allow other people's definition of success to be your guiding light. Give yourself a break from outer influences, like social media and the news.

I challenge you to write your own definition of success and happiness. Be fulfilled in yourself. Don't look for satisfaction or happiness somewhere else. When your fulfillment and happiness are tied to others, (husband, family, sorority, friends) the day they disappoint you is the day you cease to be happy. It simply means they can control your mood, and that is a dangerous authority for anyone to possess.

Everyday I look at myself in the mirror, and she is my competition. Strive to be a better you than you were yesterday, and even a better version of you tomorrow than today. Thrive on aspirations and don't lose focus on improving yourself. It is only through this you can truly compete with yourself.

> **COMPETING WITH OTHERS BREEDS ENVY & QUENCHES YOUR TRUE IDENTITY.**

"95% of the people criticizing what you do can't do what you do. The other 4% are jealous that they are not you and the 1% that really matter are either supporting you or too busy minding their own business to notice you. Don't get discouraged by what people say because your critics are always in the crowd."

Felix Anderson

9
CELEBRATE YOUR SCARS

"Each life is made up of mistakes and learning, waiting and growing, practicing patience and being persistent."

Billy Graham

To have a scar or scars means one must have been injured. The mark left by the healed wound is the scar. In life's journey, the situation might not have smiled on you, as a matter of fact, you might have gone from one injury to another. The scars begin to mar our beauty, life and leave marks on our body and memory.

When we see these marks, we remember the encounter that led to the pain. We remember what happened and how much hurt it left in our heart. A scar is a healed wound. Which means the pain and hurt is healed, necessary forgiveness has taken place.

TABATHA PITTMAN

Your scars are your mistakes. Scars might be caused by you or people who contribute to your life. When you realize your mistake and learn from it, it teaches you more because it was experienced. There is a huge difference between what you read and what you experience. The difference is reality.

Now that you have learned, you are more likely to make better choices than the former ones you made. You realize that you need to be more patient with yourself and others and weigh your options accordingly.

You can celebrate your scars by forgiving yourself of any fault you think you might have contributed. Be at peace with who you currently are and make lemonade, lemon zest, even lemon oil out of the lemons life gave you.

I have found that in in order to fully embrace your scars you must exercise the *SHOWUP* factor, *Spiritually Healthy Overcoming Woman United for Purpose.* **S**- Spiritually and emotionally you must walk in wholeness and integrity, casting off weakness and dispelling despair. **H**-Healthy in your physical and mental state, meaning you exercise for strength and choose to live in the truth. You have served a cease and desist order on illusions; and you refuse to pretend all is well when it is not. You have effectively done business with the Holy Spirit and exchanged blame (yourself or others) for responsibility, fear for freedom and false living for reality. **O-** Overcoming the obstacles and stumbling blocks the enemy sent to steal, kill and destroy you. You have mastered prevailing in the midst of adversity, trials and tribulations. As an overcomer you walk heavy in your God-given authority. You know that Gods guidance is the secret key to overcoming all the fiery darts the enemy has sent and that you are more than a conqueror. **W-** Woman of Excellence. Woman of God's wisdom excelling in your responsibilities and endeavors. You care for your household, bless your family, have a superior business mind and minister with the anointing of the Holy Ghost. In essence you are the wise woman who builds her house, and not the foolish woman who plucks it down with her own hands (Proverbs 14:1). **U-** United and aligned with what the Bible decrees and declares about you. You are married and devout, following God with relentless faith and obedience. **P-** Purpose is birthed out of your individuality. You are whole and healthy and your husband (husband to be) is a compliment to your purpose. You embrace and love you and that is the place of purpose. Your purpose is full of value and substance ready to impact the world.

"I discovered my purpose when I allowed God to show me who I was and what I need to do in order to become who He wanted me to be; from there I was able to be me with purpose & on purpose."

~

Tabatha Pittman

10
LOVE YOURSELF

"To fall in love with yourself is the first secret to happiness."

~Robert Morley

The power of self-love cannot be underestimated. It takes "you" to love you. No matter how much your family and loved ones profess to love you; you need to love and accept yourself. Know the kind of person you are. Know your temperament and how you express your personality.

Loving yourself triggers happiness, peace, contentment, love, and every positive energy that you need. It helps you to accept and understand others. More importantly, it helps you not to deny yourself of good things.

Loving yourself will aid you to know what is good for you, and you can thereby say yes to it. Many people cannot have a successful relationship because they haven't learned to first love themselves. Some don't even know what they want, much less be able to love themselves or anyone else.

You appreciate yourself by giving yourself the best. Spend time with yourself, discovering awesome things about who you are. The truth is, you can't be totally satisfied with someone loving you when you haven't loved yourself.

I have often treated myself to fine dining. I have walked right in to a five star restaurant armed with my purse, a book and the good Lord as my esteemed guest of honor. I learned that silence truly is golden and I enjoyed it. I learned that my time alone did not mean lonely. Lonely eludes to being estranged from others and deficient to couple or socialize with people. Whereas, alone is about being in solitude and loving my own company. It is a place of peace, and a rich inner life that is valued and admired. I encourage you to shift toward alone with the understanding of it being necessary to replenish and renew yourself.

> *"Love yourself. Enough to take the actions required for your happiness. Enough to cut yourself loose from the drama-filled past. Enough to set a high standard for relationships. Enough to feed your mind*

and body in a healthy manner. Enough to forgive yourself. Enough to move on."

Steve Maraboli

> MAKE AN APPOINTMENT WITH YOURSELF TO PRACTICE SELF-CARE.

WAYS TO SHOW YOURSELF LOVE

One of my favorite sayings is "you can't pour from an empty cup." It's an adage that rings true in our fast paced, everchanging world- and in order to be the Wife of Favor who is healed, happy and healthy, you have to care for yourself first. Afterall, self care is soul care. This makes it easier to share love and compassion with everyone else in your life. Let's try these on for size: banish negative self-talk, amplify kindness, and refill the self-love tank that empowers all the other hats you wear.

Self-care you can implement:

1. Do something You love everyday
2. Watch the sunrise
3. Start a gratitude journal

4. Laugh out loud, often

5. Unplug from technology

6. Blast your favorite song and dance

7. Make a home cooked meal

> *"Love is patient, love is kind. It does not envy, or does not boast, it is not proud. It is not rude, it is not self-seeking, it is not easily angered, it keeps no record of wrongs."*
>
> 1 Corinthians 13: 4-5

"You can't please, fix, help or love people until you fix, help and love yourself. Self awareness is not selfishness"

Pastor Hart Ramsey

PART THREE

SHOWING UP AS A WOMAN OF WISDOM

11
NEVER GIVE IT ONE MORE TRY

> *"Her husband can trust her, and she will greatly enrich his life."*
>
> Proverbs 31:11

The act of marriage is a forever commitment. As a prudent woman, the fruit your marriage produces is determined by how much labor you put into it; it makes it a successful and lasting marriage.

It becomes the responsibility of you and your spouse to make your marriage a success. This success is determined by the vision and mission you set forth in the beginning. The Bible teaches us that my people perish for lack of knowledge or vision. So by all mean, if you do not have a mission statement for your marriage take time with your spouse and make that top priority.

Each of you contribute to the state of your marriage. Though your personality, upbringing, and perspectives might be different, since you've committed to love and stay together forever, it is in your hands how successful the marriage will be.

TABATHA PITTMAN

As a woman, filled with God's wisdom, you are to portray yourself, not in pretense, to be invaluable to your spouse. It takes a wise woman to build a house, but the foolish one destroys it with her own hands. Let your virtues be evident in your relationship and marriage. It is through the godly characteristics you portray that your spouse will be able to trust you.

He becomes confident in his woman because he knows his secret is safe with his confidant, his helpmeet. The problem is some women don't know how to keep their lips sealed. Their mouths are like running faucets. They spill the secrets and inner heart of their husband and home, all in the hope of making friends and seeking sympathy. Not realizing that they are also betraying his trust.

When all your home business becomes community knowledge, know that as a woman, you are not doing your job well. Protect your home from scavengers. Everyone is not your friend; some are wolves in sheep's clothing. Backstabbers. Quietly you are giving the blueprint to your husband on social media rants, and fake friends who are not praying for God to intercede on your behalf. Pray over your spouse and children. A man can easily trust his woman when he knows that she goes to

God on every matter. His confidence is that he has a woman who loves him and prays for him.

The "one more chance" mentality doesn't make a marriage work. A lot of people say things like I'm going to counseling and then if that does not work I'm done. That is the wrong approach. Marriage is not a bed of roses. Obstacles are going to come, but you must continue to chase after what you want. Accept that difficulties may get in the way but determine in your heart that you will find a way to get over or go around it; but quitting is not an option. Remember also, that Paul told us in 1 Corinthians 7: 28 that "those who marry will face many troubles in this life." Therefore, we can conclude that easy street was not promised, and successful relationships take time and effort.

You must try your best, again and again, be watchful and prayerful. Be diligent and hardworking at your marriage. Be a support system for your spouse. I do my best to be my husband's sanctuary. A place where he can come and find peace and not nagging. I often say be his peace and his piece.

Never keep trying to make him better through your advice, push, and prayer. I want to share my experience in this area. I learned that the more I prayed that God would fix my husband; the more the Holy Spirit would turn the spotlight on me. When

TABATHA PITTMAN

we point the finger at him we have four other fingers pointing back at us. God worked on me. This is where I began to see that my vertical relationship with the Lord gave me a fresh lens on my horizontal relationship with my husband. I began to see him as God sees him. He is God's son just like you are God's daughter, treat him accordingly.

The commitment you made to each other before Christ should drive you to do more. Let the love between you continue to glow. Always look and pray for the good of your spouse because if he prospers, you prosper.

> *"Wives, in the same way submit yourselves to your own husbands so that, if any of them do not believe the word, they may be won over without words by the behavior of their wives, when they see the purity and reverence of your lives. Your beauty should not come from outward adornment, such as elaborate hairstyles and the wearing of gold jewelry or fine clothes. Rather, it should be that of your inner self, the unfading beauty of a gentle and quiet spirit, which is of great worth in God's sight. For this is the way the holy women of the*

THE FAVOR OF A WIFE

past who put their hope in God used to adorn themselves. They submitted themselves to their own husbands, like Sarah, who obeyed Abraham and called him her Lord. You are her daughters if you do what is right and do not give way to fear."

1 Peter 3:1-6

Marriage is the most sophisticated of all relationships. It is a shame that so many put more effort into the wedding day than they do their actual marriage. Never give up on your marriage, because when you do you give up on yourself! (I am not suggesting you stay in a marriage that is laden with abuse or adultery.) Maybe you are reading this and thinking you have done all you can do or even implemented other suggestions that I have already listed. If so, I invite you to continue reading and keep praying.

I want to share some of the tips and tools I have learned after being married nine years at the time of this publication. One of the first things that I noticed was we seemed to argue about the same things, frustration would build and communication would cease. It was a crazy vicious cycle. I was blaming him for not meeting my needs, and in doing so I was reacting with disrespect.

TABATHA PITTMAN

Without respect a man reacts without love. Neither of our needs were being met, leaving the marriage in an emotional deficit. Next, I complained a lot about him being a workaholic and not spending enough time with me. Nagging never helps. He would retaliate that this was his career, which he was in when we met. Lastly, as a result we were not talking because my feelings were hurt and he was feeling unappreciated. It has been said when a husband and wife are not talking to each other, the devil is talking to both of you. For most women, not communicating may also mean not being physically intimate or refusing sex.

My marriage was spiraling out of control fast. This was not how I dreamed marriage would be. I immediately began to read everything I could get my hands on to help me understand. The world teaches from kindergarten to college the necessary skills to be contributing members of society with a job or career but there is no education provided on how to sustain, maintain, or achieve a successful marriage. For this reason learning all you can in this arena is vital to matrimony. You can start with the Bible.

What I am about to share is wisdom for every woman: If not for you now, then certainly your daughter, future daughter-in-law, niece, or grandchild later. I am grateful that I was able to gather this information, through much prayer, trial and error, with my ring and heart still intact.

Wise Wife Wisdom (5W³)

1. **Respect and Honor** are to your husband what love is to you. He does value your love but he interprets it R.E.S.P.E.C.T.
    a. **Wife To Do:** Genuinely tell him you respect him.

2. **His work is part of his Identity and Achievement.** God made him to work (see Genesis 2:15) and to provide for his family, that's You. Do not criticize his work.
    a. **Wife To Do:** As much as you want to hear he loves you, say, "Thank you and I appreciate you."
    b. **Wife To Do:** Listen attentively to him no matter how many times he tells the same work story.

3. **Praise him for his willingness to provide and protect.** This is a part of his DNA.
    a. **Wife To Do:** Make sure he knows you do not take his commitment to provide for granted.
    b. **Wife To Do:** Never criticize his job or how much money he makes.

4. **Trust him as the head of household.** Read Ephesians 5:21-22 and verse 33 as a reminder of the mutual submission required. *A refusal to submit and respect is equivalent to a refusal to trust God.
    a. **Wife To Do:** Acknowledge that he is The Man, the leader, the one in charge and responsible before God.

b. **Wife To Do:** Defer to him as the pastor having 51% and you being assistant pastor at 49%. Honor his authority in front of kids and others and disagree in private.

c. **Wife To Do:** Give grace for his bad decisions and praise for the good decisions.

5. **Recognize that you are not his Holy Spirit; there is no vacancy in the Trinity.**

    a. **Wife To Do:** Discern and denounce any spirit of self-righteousness and pride in you that may undermine his position.

    b. **Wife To Do:** Thank him for his advice and fix-it approach as his way of empathizing with you.

Now this list certainly is not all inclusive but it is a place to start applying God's wisdom, shifting your perception of your spouse and annihilating the "one more chance" mentality.

12

FREEDOM FROM UNREALISTIC EXPECTATIONS

Everything and everyone shouldn't have your attention. Create balance in your life by saying "NO" to anything and anyone not in alignment with your purpose.

Many marriages were built on fables and pleasures. Some ladies run after wealthy men and even sometimes divorce them so that they can inherit the assets. This is the wisdom of the world. The fact that a man can lavish his wealth on you doesn't mean he is someone you can make a home with.

Because of the nature of Christian marriage and knowing that God hates divorce, it is critical to choose wisely and for those who have chosen, live life based on God's wisdom. Don't be lured with money; because a day might come that both him and the money are gone. A lot of hurt advise may say to marry for money; but, let it be known that love may not pay the bills however it can keep a happy home.

There is a lot of enticement and entanglement greatly used to deceive and ensnare you. For this reason the Bible says godliness with contentment is a great gain. The love of money has entrapped some women into wrong relationships and marriage. They believed with money; there is no problem that won't be solved. They believe there will be a status upgrade, and the marriage will last. They chose to serve mamon, the god of money. I'm here to tell you the character of a man is what is more sustainable. You can acquire money and wealth, but the Bible says what profits a man to gain the whole world and lose his soul?

Material or temporary things don't make a successful marriage. It is only a benchmark if you begin to judge your home in comparison with the standard of the world. Seeking materialistic gain is a temporary patch, when Jesus is the only way to fill the void and bring true peace.

Most women make a common mistake to set standards, high hopes, and world class expectations pertaining to their marriage. Even when it is rosy at first, you have not laid a good foundation for stormy weather and times. These unrealistic expectations cloud the mind that when things aren't going as planned, they immediately start to complain and look for alternative outlets. That is why it is said that marriage is not for kids. Love requires sacrifice not selfishness. If you want to see the success you have to put in the work, and make the sacrifice that is required. You make the time to have date night. Know that unrealistic expectations lead you on an empty quest down a bunny hole. But shifting your mindset to see marriage as a project and a process where you extend grace, mercy and patience. Walk in forgiveness and love as Christ did for us.

Many events occur in a marriage that are unplanned, but the wisdom of God is profitable to direct you so that you know what to do in every circumstance. It is good to have expectations, but they must be realistic. The worst thing you can do is be too ambitious or try to keep up with the Jones' and find yourself living outside of your means and outside the will of God. Additionally, trying to keep up with anyone or covet what they have is giving a foot hold for comparison and strongman influence in your marriage and household.

Be ready to play your part by making the right choice and not setting unrealistic expectations for your spouse. For instance, you know your household's financial strength and that it is not resilient enough, but you insist on going on an expensive vacation or buying jewelry, which is not important to your life at the moment.

Living an unrealistic dream is living under pretense and frustration. Don't compete with anyone. Let the things you do be done under moderation and always rely on God to lead you.

As you embrace this journey and begin to traverse the landscape of marriage, keep these words, declarations, principles, and prayers in mind and allow them to be your source of inspiration and motivation.

The 3 F's To Expect When You Awaken Your Favor as a Wife

1. Expect to be equipped with FAVOR that will help catapult you to your next level in your marriage.
2. A new level of laser FOCUS to help you with your next level. Focus on listening, making memories, and connecting spiritually.
3. Expect to have FRUITFUL opportunities presented to you as you reach your next level.

Prayer to Bless Our Marriage

THE FAVOR OF A WIFE

We thank You, Lord, for the love You have implanted in my heart and husband's heart. May It always inspire us to only speak in kindness and respect. I ask You Lord, to show me how to be considerate of his feelings and always be concerned for his needs and wishes. Help me to be understanding and forgiving of his weaknesses and feelings. Bless this marriage, O'Lord, with peace and happiness, and make our love fruitful so that we will be an example of Your Glory and Joy to others on this earth and in eternity. Lord I ask for this marriage blessing in Jesus Name. Amen

RING THE ALARM

It's time for you to WALK IN THE FAVOR OF A WIFE and live your dreams. It's time for you to WALK IN THE FAVOR OF A WIFE and be who and what you are purposed to be.

Stop seeking permission from people to be great as a woman and wife. God created you in His image and likeness so greatness is in You. God has filled your life with good things and you can trust Him. Don't accept stumbling or destruction. You are destined for Royalty. You are destined for greatness. Greatness is on the inside of you and your next level as a

Wife of Favor is right around the corner.

In closing, it is my desire that every reader is spiritually fit and has the capacity to do what God has assigned to you. My purpose was to activate the Favor of a Wife that may have been dormant in you. I am on assignment to speak to the woman in you that may have been on autopilot, to bring your vertical relationship in alignment with God so that your horizontal relationships come into proper perspective. I pray that you will exercise your faith muscle and trust God to rule you, your spouse and your marriage. Doing such is a decision to surrender to God's unfailing love and plan for your life. God is your source. I humbly request that you apply these principles and watch the success of oneness come to fruition in your relationship with your husband as a **Wife of Favor**.

ABOUT THE AUTHOR

Tabatha Pittman is a certified Life and Relationship Coach from Michigan, USA. A devout Christian and minister of the faith, she has long dedicated her life to motivating and inspiring people to seek God's truth and pursue their life's passions through faith in Jesus. She is the CEO of Tabatha Pittman Coaching & Consulting LLC, an avenue through which she continues to encourage and empower others to build and live their best lives personally and in the marketplace. Embracing her excellence, she also serves as a full-time mother and wife who loves spending quality time with her family, reading, and enjoying a healthy work out from time to time.

www.ingramcontent.com/pod-product-compliance
Lightning Source LLC
Chambersburg PA
CBHW050916160426
43194CB00011B/2430